12/99

GETTING TO KNOW THE WORLD'S GREATEST ARTISTS

FRIDA
KAHLO

WRITTEN AND ILLUSTRATED BY MIKE VENEZIA

CHILDREN'S PRESS®
A DIVISION OF GROLIER PUBLISHING
NEW YORK   LONDON   HONG KONG   SYDNEY
DANBURY, CONNECTICUT

For Mike and Liz

Cover: *Self-Portrait with Monkey,* by Frida Kahlo. 1940. © Art Resource, NY.

Library of Congress Cataloging-in-Publication Data

Venezia, Mike.
   Frida Kahlo / written and illustrated by Mike Venezia.
      p. cm. — (Getting to know the world's greatest artists)
   Summary: Discusses the life of Mexican painter Frida Kahlo,
including her childhood, her art, and her marriage to Diego Rivera.
   ISBN 0-516-20975-2 (lib. bdg.)   0-516-26466-4 (pbk.)
   1. Kahlo, Frida—Juvenile literature. 2. Painters—Mexico—
Biography—Juvenile literature. [1. Kahlo, Frida. 2. Artists.
3. Women—Biography.] I. Title. II. Series: Venezia, Mike.
Getting to know the world's greatest artists.
ND259.K33V46 1999
759.972—dc21
[B]   98-29580
                                        CIP
                                        AC

Visit Children's Press on the Internet at:
http://publishing.grolier.com

Frida Kahlo was one of the greatest
Mexican artists of the twentieth century.
She was born in Coyoacán, Mexico, in
1907. Frida grew up during the Mexican
Revolution, an event that influenced her
life and changed the art of Mexico forever.

Self-Portrait Dedicated to Leon Trotsky, by Frida Kahlo. 1937. Oil on masonite. 30 x 20 in.
© The National Museum of Women in the Arts, Gift of the Honorable Clare Booth Luce.

Some of Frida's most famous works are self-portraits. In many of them she shows herself surrounded by things that were important to her.

Frida especially liked
to paint flowers, plants,
forests, animals,
costumes, jewelry, and
ancient gods and
idols that were found
only in Mexico.

Frida often showed unpleasant things that happened during her life. These paintings are sometimes shocking to people. But Frida needed to paint them to help her get through some hard times.

The painting shown on the next page, *Without Hope,* was done after a serious illness. Frida had grown weak and had no appetite. Her doctors wanted her to eat lots of strained foods. Frida was disgusted by the idea of being forced to eat, and showed how she felt about this in her painting. Frida painted most of these disturbing pictures for herself. She was surprised when anyone else showed any interest in them.

Sin Esperanza (Without Hope), by Frida Kahlo. 1945. Photograph © Schalkwijk/Art Resource, NY.

Frida Kahlo went through a lot of pain and suffering during her life. When she was five years old, she caught a serious disease called polio. She got better, but the disease left her right leg thin and weak.

To help improve her leg, Frida's parents got her to do lots of physical activities, including soccer, swimming, bicycling, and even boxing!

From left to right: Frida, her grandmother, her sister Adriana and her husband Carlos Veraza, her uncle, her mother, and a cousin, Cristina Kahlo. 1926. Guillermo Kahlo. © Reproduction authorized by Instituto Nacional de Bellas Artes y Literatura/Centro Nacional de las Artes, Biblioteca de las Artes, Mexico.

Nothing seemed to help, though. Kids in the neighborhood started calling her "Frida peg leg." Frida wore long dresses and pants to hide her leg. She never wanted anyone to know she was different, or feel sorry for her, or make fun of her.

Frida Kahlo was very curious as a child. She especially wanted to know about nature and science. Her father thought this was great, and encouraged Frida to learn as much as she could.

El Castillo Chichén Itzá (Mayan), Yucatan, Mexico.
Photograph © Superstock, Inc.

Frida was always bringing home plants, rocks, insects, and small animals to study. Mr. Kahlo was a professional photographer and an amateur artist who was also curious about all kinds of things. He taught his daughter about ancient Mexican art and architecture. Mr. Kahlo showed Frida how to use a camera and how to retouch and color photographs. These things came in handy later, when Frida became an artist.

Frida attended one of the best high schools in the country. It was located right in the middle of Mexico City. In high school, Frida learned how important the Mexican Revolution was to the people of her country.

Zapata's Agrarian Revolution, by David Alfaro Siqueiros. Fresco. Museo Nacional de Historia, Mexico City. Photograph © Giraudon/Art Resource, NY.

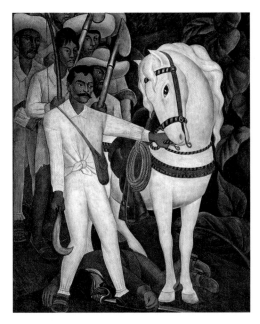

Agrarian Leader Zapata, by Diego Rivera. 1931. Fresco. 238.1 x 188 cm. Abby Aldrich Rockefeller Fund. © Museum of Modern Art, New York.

Before the Revolution, thousands of people were treated like slaves. They were very poor and uneducated, and most worked on farms all day long. A few greedy government officials and farm owners kept all the money for themselves.

In 1910, the Mexican people, with leaders like Pancho Villa and Emiliano Zapata, rebelled against the Mexican government and won the right to make life fair for everyone in Mexico.

Triumph of the Revolution-Distribution of Food (Triunfo de la Revolución, reparto de los alimentos), by Diego Rivera. 1926-27. Fresco. 3.54 x 3.67 m. Chapel, Universidad Autónoma Chapingo, Chapingo, Mexico. Photograph © Schalkwijk/Art Resource, NY.

The Trench, by José Clemente Orozco. Escuela Nacional Preparatoria San Ildefonso, Mexico City, Mexico. Photograph © Schalkwijk/Art Resource, NY.

Huelga de Cananea, by David Alfaro Siqueiros. Museo Nacional de Historia, Castillo de Chapultepec, Mexico City, Mexico. Photograph © Schalkwijk/Art Resource, NY.

One of the first things the new Mexican government did was hire artists to paint large scenes on the walls of public buildings for everyone to see. These paintings, called murals, showed the history of Mexico. They were meant to help uneducated people understand their past, make them proud of their country, and give them hope for the future.

The Totonac Civilization, by Diego Rivera. 1942. Mural. 4.92 x 5.27 m. Patio Corridor, National Palace, Mexico City, Mexico. Photograph © Schalkwijk/Art Resource, NY.

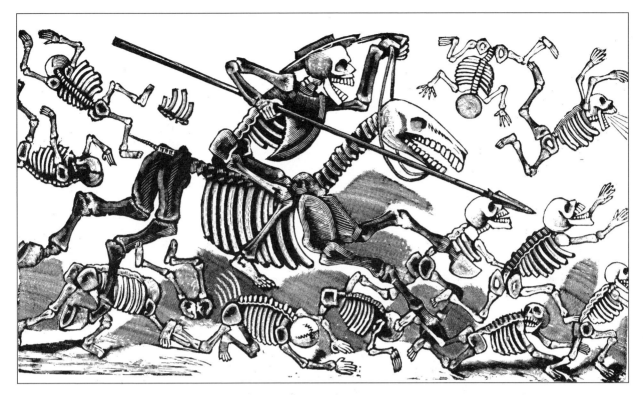

Calavera de Don Quijote, by José Guadalupe Posada. Engraving. © Posada's Popular Mexican Prints, 1972, Dover Publications.

The most famous mural artists were David Siqueiros, José Orozco, and Diego Rivera. These painters were inspired by the art and colors of ancient Mexican civilizations. They were also influenced by Mexican popular art, like the lively prints of José Posada. They purposely kept away from European-influenced art, which was the accepted style of art before the Mexican Revolution.

Creation, by Diego Rivera. Fresco. Escuela Nacional Preparatoria, Anfiteatro Bolívar, Mexico City, Mexico. Photograph © Detroit Institute of Arts.

When Frida was fourteen years old, Diego Rivera came to her school to paint one of his murals. In high school, Frida was known as a troublemaker. She made herself a pain in the

neck to her teachers and anyone else in authority, including the famous Diego. Frida played tricks on Diego and called out names, like "old fatso," while he was trying to work.

El accidente 17 de septiembre de 1926, by Frida Kahlo. 1926. Pencil on paper. 20 x 27 cm. Colección Rafael Coronel. © Reproduction authorized by Instituto Nacional de Bellas Artes y Literatura/Centro Nacional de las Artes, Biblioteca de las Artes, Mexico.

Frida wasn't all that interested in art until a very bad thing happened to her. One day, on the way home from school, the bus she was riding got into a terrible accident. Some people were even killed. Frida was badly injured and had to spend months in bed. Her bones never really healed properly. She had lots of pain and had to have many operations during her life.

It was at this time that Frida decided to take up art. She was bored lying in bed and needed something to do. Frida borrowed her father's paints and brushes. Her mother had a special easel made so Frida could work

while she was lying on her back. Frida started by painting portraits of her friends, family, and the subject she knew best: herself.

Autorretrato, by Frida Kahlo. 1926. Oil on masonite. 78 x 61 cm. Colección Instituto Tlaxcalteca de Cultura, Tlaxcala, Mexico. © Reproduction authorized by Instituto Nacional de Bellas Artes y Literatura/Centro Nacional de las Artes, Biblioteca de las Artes, Mexico.

At first, Frida was her own teacher. She studied her father's art books and copied the paintings of great European artists like Botticelli and Modigliani. But soon, just like the Mexican mural artists, Frida became more interested in the folk art of her own country. Frida loved the energy of these works of art and the simple stories they told.

These paintings and prints seemed filled with the magic that many people in Mexico felt was a real part of their everyday lives. She found a mysterious power in religious paintings and ancient Mexican Indian art. Frida began to include in her own paintings the things that she discovered in Mexican folk art.

The Bus (El Camion), by Frida Kahlo. 1929. Oil on canvas. 26 x 55 cm. Fundación Dolores Olmedo, Mexico City, D. F., Mexico. Photograph © Schalkwijk/ Art Resource, NY.

Birth of Class Consciousness (El Agitador), by Diego Rivera. 1926-27. Mural. 2.44 x 5.53 m. Chapel, Universidad Autónoma Chapingo, Chapingo, Mexico. Photograph © Schalkwijk/Art Resource, NY.

Frida enjoyed painting. It made her feel better. Soon she felt well enough to get around again. Frida made up her mind then never to let her pain and injuries get in the way of having fun. She kept working on her paintings, got together with friends, and went to lots of parties.

At one party, she was introduced to Diego Rivera. He didn't remember Frida because she was grown up now and looked much different.

Diego did remember her, though, a few days later, when she came to see him while he was painting one of his murals. Frida wanted to show Diego some of her artwork to see what he thought. Even though Frida had teased him years before, she had always been fascinated by Diego and respected his talent.

Diego thought Frida's artwork was great. Now that Frida was grown up, he thought she was great, too. Frida invited Diego to her home to look at other paintings she had done.

Diego visited the Kahlo home often. He and Frida got to know each other well and started dating. After a while, they fell in love. Even though Diego was more than twenty years older than Frida, they decided to get married.

Frida Kahlo and Diego Rivera. 1931. Photograph © Peter Juley. Colección Museo Frida Kahlo
© Reproduction authorized by Instituto Nacional de Bellas Artes y Literatura/Centro
Nacional de las Artes, Biblioteca de las Artes, Mexico.

Diego always encouraged Frida with her art. He was proud of his talented wife. Frida learned a lot from Diego. He turned out to be an excellent art teacher.

Now Frida Kahlo was the wife of one of the most famous artists in the world. At first it was fine with her to just take care of her husband. Frida enjoyed being with Diego every day while he worked. But she wasn't doing much of her own artwork.

In the 1930s, Diego was asked to paint murals in the United States. Diego and Frida traveled there often and were admired wherever they went. They looked great together and were fun to be around. Frida and

Diego were always being invited to the parties of rich and famous people.

Frida and Diego Rivera, by Frida Kahlo. 1931. Oil on canvas. 100 x 78.7 cm. Albert M. Bender Collection.
Gift of Albert M. Bender. © San Francisco Museum of Modern Art.

Things didn't always go well between Diego and Frida, though. They often had serious arguments. One disagreement was over how much time they were spending in the United States. Diego loved the modern American cities, but Frida didn't enjoy being there at all. She was homesick and wanted to get back to Mexico.

Frida did the painting on the next page to show her feelings about the United States. She painted an overcrowded New York City filled with factories, garbage, and pollution. There's no sign of Frida in this picture. She has probably returned to Mexico, leaving only her dress behind.

My Dress Hangs Here, by Frida Kahlo. 1933-38. © Christie's Images/Superstock, Inc.

Sometimes, after a serious argument, Frida and Diego would live apart from each other. During these times, Frida painted more often, and created some of her best works.

Frida Kahlo painted her real feelings in a way that had never been seen before. As time went on, her work started to become as well known as her famous husband's. Frida was able to show her happiness, disappointment, and pain. Her paintings are filled with Mexican colors and images that could have come only from someone who loved their country as much as she did.

The Frame, by Frida Kahlo. Centre National d'Art et de Culture Georges Pompidou, Paris
© Musée National D'Art Moderne.

Frida Kahlo's health was a serious problem throughout her life. She died in 1954. But early on, Frida had decided to enjoy life as much as possible. She always spent a lot of time fixing her hair and dressing in beautiful costumes. Some of her friends said that when she was finished, she had become almost a piece of art herself.

Photograph of Frida Kahlo, by Nickolas Muray.
© Nickolas Muray /George Eastman House.

Works of art in this book can be seen at the following places:

Escuela Nacional Preparatoria San Ildefonso, Mexico City, Mexico
Instituto Tlaxcalteca de Cultura, Tlaxcala, Mexico
Musée National d'Art Moderne, Paris, France
Museo Frida Kahlo, Mexico City, Mexico
Museo Nacional de Arte Moderno, Mexico City, Mexico
Museo Nacional de Historia, Mexico City, Mexico
The Museum of Modern Art, New York, New York
National Gallery of Art, Washington, D.C.
National Museum of Women in the Arts, Washington, D.C.
National Palace, Mexico City, Mexico
San Antonio Museum of Art, San Antonio, Texas
San Francisco Museum of Modern Art, San Francisco, California
Universidad Autonoma Chapingo, Chapingo, Mexico